MW01104977

Scripture quotations are taken from the Holy Bible, New Living Translation, copyright © 1996. Used by permission of Tyndale House Publishers, Inc. Wheaton, Illinois 60189. All rights reserved.

© 2001 Carolyn Larsen.

New Kids Media™ is published by Baker Book House Company, Grand Rapids, Michigan.

ISBN 0-8010-4472-3

Printed in China.

1 2 3 4 5 6 7 — 04 03 02 01

Little Boys Tiny Bible Storybook

Carolyn Larsen
Illustrated by Caron Turk

BAKER
A DIVISION OF
Baker Book House Co

Contents

That's What Little Boys are Made Of

The bear was eating honey when the earth started shaking. He dove behind a rock and peeked out at the swirling dust. God himself was moving the dirt, shaping it into his best creation. . . . Adam, the very first man.

Adam stretched his arms and wiggled his fingers. Everything worked! He ran through the garden, skipped stones on a lake, and climbed a tree. But a while later, he slumped on the ground. "What's wrong?" God asked.

"I don't know. I guess I'm bored," Adam sighed.

"Well, how would you like to give names to the animals?" God asked. The animals marched by Adam and he gave each one a name. But when he finished he plopped down on the ground again.

"I know what the problem is," God said. "You're lonely! You need someone to talk to who is more like you than the animals are." God made Adam sleep and he took one of Adam's ribs to make Eve, the first woman.

You will be best friends..... ♥

"Wake up," God whispered. Adam opened his eyes and saw a beautiful new creature. "This is Eve," God said. "She will be your friend and your wife. You both are a lot like me. You can think, talk, and make decisions. I know you'll be very happy together."

Based on Genesis 1–2

Becoming a Man of God

A man of God knows he is made in God's image.

Adam and Eve were made in God's image. That means they were a lot like him. They were the first humans. You're a human, too, so that means you are also made in God's image.

What do you know about God? He is loving, kind, honest and fair. Since we are made in God's image, we should be loving, kind, honest and fair, too.

Grown-up Time

Tell your little boy some of your favorite things to do. Does he enjoy doing any of those things, too?

Think about someone who has interests different from yours or who is good at other kinds of things. Remind your little boy that every person is different, but we are all made in God's image. He made each of us to be exactly like he wants us to be.

A Verse to Remember
As the Spirit of the Lord works within us, we become more and more like him and reflect his glory even more.
2 Corinthians 3:18

One Big Happy Family

"Let me outta here!" Joseph shouted. He tried to climb out of the hole where his brothers had thrown him. They hated him because he was their dad's favorite. Dad had even given Joseph a fancy coat like rich people wore.

When the brothers saw some men going to
Egypt, one brother said, "Let's sell Joseph to be
a slave in Egypt. We'll make some money and
get rid of him. We'll tell Dad that a wild
animal killed him."

Joseph was a good slave for Potiphar. He was put in charge of the whole house. But one day Mrs. Potiphar got mad because Joseph wouldn't do what she wanted him to do. So she told some lies and Joseph ended up in jail.

The other prisoners made fun of Joseph because he prayed every day. But when God helped Joseph explain Pharaoh's dreams, Pharaoh was so thankful that he made Joseph second in command over the whole country.

One day Joseph's brothers came to Egypt to buy food. They didn't recognize him, but he knew them! He could have gotten even with them for the bad things they did to him, but he didn't. Instead he said, "It's me, Joseph. I forgive you for hurting me." That's exactly what God wanted him to do!

Based on Genesis 37–45

Becoming a Man of God

A man of God forgives.

Joseph could have tried to pay back his brothers for being so mean to him. But he loved God and he knew God wanted him to be kind and forgiving.

Has anyone ever done something mean to you? How did you feel? Did you want to get even with them?

Grown-up Time

Have you ever been hurt by someone? How did you feel? Did you forgive that person or try to get even?

Remind your little boy how Jesus forgave people who were mean to him. Thank God that he is always willing to forgive us for the wrong things we do.

A Verse to Remember
Even if he wrongs you seven times a day and each time turns again and asks forgiveness, forgive him.
Luke 17:4

Red Sea PANIC

The Egyptian army was chasing the
Israelites and the people were shouting at
Moses. "What's going to happen to us? Did
you bring us out of Egypt to die here in the
desert? We should have stayed in Egypt!"

No wonder the people were confused. God had done ten miracles to get them out of Egypt, but now Pharaoh's army wanted to bring them back to Egypt to be slaves again. The Israelites were trapped with their backs to the Red Sea.

Moses poured out his heart to God. "Are my people going to die here? Are we going to be dragged back to slavery? What's going on?" Of course, God had a plan. He didn't bring them to the desert just to let bad things happen. God told Moses exactly what to do.

"Watch what God will do to save you,"
Moses called to the people. He raised
his hand over the water and a
strong wind began to blow. It
blew harder and harder until the
water blew apart, making two big walls with
a dry path between them.

One brave man stepped between the water walls, then everyone followed and all the Israelites crossed the Red Sea. When the Egyptian soldiers followed them, the water crashed down and drowned every soldier. But every Israelite was safe.

Based on Exodus 14

Becoming a Man of God
A man of God works for God.

Remember when God first asked Moses to do his work? Moses was scared. He didn't think he could do it. But when Moses understood that God would help him, he was willing to do God's work.

Have you ever had to do something that was scary or hard? Why was it scary? Were you able to do it?

Grown-up Time

Tell your little boy about a time when you
had to something that was very difficult for
you. Why was it hard? How did you get
through it?

Talk about the way that exercising the
muscles in your body makes them stronger.
It's the same way with our spiritual muscles.
Trusting God to help us do hard things makes
our faith grow stronger.

A Verse to Remember
I can do everything with the help of Christ
who gives me the strength I need.
Philippians 4:13

No Fear!

King Saul's soldiers were scared of Goliath, a giant Philistine soldier who kept shouting, "Send one soldier out to fight me. Winner takes all!" No one would go. "I'm not scared of the big ugly giant," David said firmly.

Suddenly David's older brother grabbed his shoulder and shouted, "Go home, you little show-off."

"Oh, I'll go alright . . . but not home! I'm going to fight the giant!" David marched off to see King Saul.

King Saul was excited to have a volunteer until he saw that David was just a kid. "Well, at least wear my armor," he said. (He knew David didn't have a chance.) David put the armor on, but it was so heavy that he couldn't move.

"Let me out of this!" he cried. "I have to do this my way!"

David picked up a stone and put it in his slingshot. When Goliath saw young David coming to fight him, he got M-A-D! He flexed his giant muscles and pounded his spear on the ground. David still wasn't scared!

David swung his slingshot in circles over his head. At just the right moment, he let the stone fly. It landed right on Goliath's forehead and the 9-foot-tall giant fell to the ground. The Israelite soldiers cheered, "The little guy won!" But David knew that he won because God helped him.

Based on 1 Samuel 18

Becoming a Man of God
A man of God trusts God's power.

Why weren't King Saul's soldiers
brave enough to fight Goliath?
They didn't believe they had God's
power helping them. They didn't
trust God enough to believe they
could defeat the giant.

When you have to do something
very hard, do you ask God to help
you?

Grown-up Time

Does your little boy see you trust in God for help in your everyday life? That's the best way he can learn to trust God, too. Tell him about a time when you knew for sure that God was helping you in a difficult situation.

Ask your little boy if there is something he needs God's help with right now. Pray together, asking for God's help in that situation.

A Verse to Remember
The LORD is good. When trouble comes, he is a strong refuge.
Nahum 1:7

Olive Oil Overflow

"Momma, do we have to go live with that mean man?" the little boy whispered. His mother hugged him and his brother. Wasn't it enough that their father had just died? Now this man said that her husband owed him money and threatened to take her boys as slaves if she didn't pay up.

"Don't worry, honey. I won't let him take you, at least not without a fight." She knew that if anyone could help her it would be the prophet of God. So the frightened mother hurried to see Elisha. He listened carefully to the whole sad story.

"I don't have any money so I can't pay the man. All I have left is my sons. Please don't let him take my boys!" she begged Elisha. When he asked her what she had in her house, she sadly said, "Just one jar of olive oil!"

"Here's what you do," Elisha told her. "Send your sons to the neighbors to borrow all of the empty jars and bowls they can find." When the boys returned, Elisha said, "Pour your jar of oil into one of the empty jars."

"OK, this jar is full. Bring another one," she called to her sons. Jar after jar was filled to the brim from the woman's one little jar of oil.

"Now, sell all the oil and pay the man what you owe him. Use the rest of the money to buy food," Elisha said, smiling at the happy little family.

Based on 2 Kings 4:1-7

Becoming a Man of God
A man of God goes to God for help.

The woman in this story knew exactly where to go for help. God's prophet was the right person to ask. Any problem or trouble that we have is best handled by talking to God about it. The great thing to remember is that nothing happens to you without God knowing about it.

Grown-up Time

Tell your little boy about a difficult situation you have faced sometime in your life. Tell him why it was hard or painful. Tell him how you prayed about it and how God helped you through it.

Remind your little boy that God sometimes helps us by showing us what to do. Sometimes God gives us a great idea and that's how he helps us with a problem.

A Verse to Remember
If you need wisdom–if you want to know what God wants you to do–ask him, and he will gladly tell you.

James 1:5

The Fish That Didn't Get Away!

"No way! I'm not going to Nineveh!"
Jonah shouted at God. "If I tell them about
you, they'll be sorry for their sins, and you'll
forgive them. I don't like those people and
I'm not going to do it!"

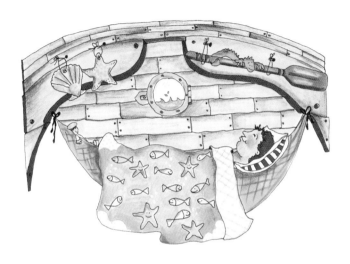

Jonah climbed on a ship headed for
Tarshish (the opposite direction of Nineveh).
He headed straight for a room in the bottom
of the ship. "God will never find me here," he
thought as he fell asleep.

Meanwhile,
the biggest
storm the sailors
had ever seen
blew up. Winds
and waves tossed the ship
around as if it were a toy. "Toss cargo
overboard! Bring in the sails!" The sailors
were scared they were going to die.

"Wake up, Jonah. If you have a god, pray for help!" a terrified sailor called. Jonah knew right away that the storm was his fault. God had found him.

"Throw me overboard and the storm will stop!" he said. The sailors didn't want to, but they were out of other ideas! So they tossed Jonah into the water.

He barely hit the water before a big fish swallowed him. For three days and nights Jonah had nothing to do but think about how he had disobeyed God. "I'm sorry I didn't obey you, God. I'll do whatever you want." Then the fish spit Jonah out and he headed straight for Nineveh.

Based on Jonah 1–4

Becoming a Man of God

A man of God obeys immediately.

Jonah should have obeyed God right away. But God gave him a second chance to do the right thing.

When someone asks you to do something, do you obey right away, or do you say, "In a minute," then never get around to doing it? When was a time that you did obey right away? When was a time that you didn't?

Grown-up Time

Tell your boy about a time when you didn't obey but later wished that you had.

Remember what it's like to be a child. Someone is always telling you what to do! Ask if there are certain things your son has trouble obeying. Recall a time when your little boy obeyed immediately. Tell him how proud you were of him. Reinforce obedience every chance you get!

A Verse to Remember
When you obey me, you remain in my love, just as I obey my Father and remain in his love.
John 15:10

A Trusting Stepdad

"God wants you to know that Mary was telling you the truth. The baby she's going to have is the Son of God, so go ahead and marry her." Joseph usually didn't have dreams about bigger-than-life angels like this one in his dream.

A few months later, Mary and Joseph were on their way to Bethlehem. The baby in Mary's tummy would be born any day and the donkey ride was very hard for her. "Are you OK, Mary?" Joseph asked. "When we get to Bethlehem, we'll get a nice room at the inn and you can rest," he promised.

The crowded, smelly streets made Mary's stomach feel sick. "Hang on, I'll get a room," Joseph promised, hurrying to the inn. A few minutes later he was back. "There aren't any rooms left in the whole town. The best we can do is sleep in the stable."

Joseph piled some clean hay together and made a bed for Mary. She fell asleep right away. But a while later she shook Joseph awake. "The baby is coming!" The stable animals were very quiet when Joseph placed little Jesus in Mary's arms.

Joseph looked up to see some shepherds leaning over the stable door. "We saw some angels and they told us that your baby is the Messiah. We came to worship him." Joseph was amazed, but Mary didn't even seem to be surprised by what they said.

Based on Matthew 1:20-25; Luke 2:1-20

Becoming a Man of God
A man of God trusts God's plan.

Joseph and Mary had been planning their wedding for a long time. They didn't expect any surprises, but the news that Mary was going to have a baby was definitely not in their plans. Joseph trusted God enough to continue with the wedding and see what happened.

Joseph was willing to keep on going, even though he didn't really know what was ahead. He knew that God did know and that was good enough for him.

Grown-up Time

Share an example from your childhood of a time
when you had to trust someone. Perhaps you
moved to a new town and you had to trust your
parents that everything would be OK.

Talk with your little boy about how it feels
when you can't do anything about a situation
yourself so you have to trust someone else.
Reinforce to your little boy that God is worthy
of our trust because he loves us.

A Verse to Remember
Trust in the LORD with all your heart; do not
depend on your own understanding.
Proverbs 3:5

"Could you push the boat
out from shore a little?"

"Who does this guy think he is?" Peter
wondered. But for some reason, he didn't
kick the guy out. In fact, he pushed the boat
out a bit and listened to the man teach the
crowd of people.

When the man finished teaching he turned to Peter and said, "Throw your nets in the water over there and you'll catch lots of fish."

"Yeah, right," Peter thought. "I've fished my whole life and this guy is telling me where to catch fish?"

"Look, we fished in that very spot all night and didn't catch a thing," Peter sighed. "We're tired and we want to go home." The stranger stared at Peter for several minutes. "OK, OK, we'll give it a try," Peter finally said.

As soon as the net hit the water it filled
with hundreds of fish . . . so many fish that
Peter and his helpers couldn't pull it in.
Peter looked at the strange man. "What's
going on?" The man just smiled and
suddenly Peter knew that this man was
special . . . holy . . . the Son of God.

Peter dropped to his knees, but Jesus pulled him to his feet. "Follow me and from now on you will fish for people," he said. Peter left his fishing boat and followed Jesus.

Based on Luke 5:1-11

Becoming a Man of God
A man of God follows Jesus.

Jesus has different jobs for each of us
to do because we are each different
people. Peter's job was to tell other
people about Jesus. He left behind his
fishing boat and fished for people.

Do you know yet what job God has for
you to do? Do you need to leave
something in your life behind, such as
selfishness or grumpiness, so that you
can do God's work?

Grown-up Time

Share your testimony with your little boy. Who led you to Christ? Who helped you grow in your faith? That person was following Christ. Discuss ways that you do God's work; teaching Sunday school, singing in choir, helping a neighbor, or making friends with people who don't know Christ.

Talk with your little boy about ways he can be a Jesus follower. Give him examples of ways he is already following Jesus.

A Verse to Remember
Come, be my disciples, and I will show you
how to fish for people!
Matthew 4:19

Bread and Fish for Everyone!

"Can I go hear Jesus speak? Please, Mom, please?" The little boy bounced around his mom, begging her to say yes.

"Well, I guess so, but let me pack a little lunch for you to take," Mom smiled at her excited little boy.

The boy sat near the front of the crowd and listened carefully to Jesus until one of Jesus' helpers said, "Master, send the people home to eat dinner."

"No," the boy thought, "teach some more, Jesus." When he heard Jesus tell the man, "No, you give them food," he almost cheered out loud.

"We have no food and no money to buy any," the man explained.

"You can have my lunch," the boy offered, holding his bag out to him.

"That little thing won't do any good," the man snapped. The boy felt silly for even offering his lunch.

A gentle hand lifted the boy's chin. Jesus smiled, took the lunch, and prayed, "Thank you, God, for this food." Then he broke the bread and fish into pieces. The disciples passed it out, and everyone had all they wanted to eat.

Jesus' helpers picked up twelve baskets of leftovers. "There must have been 5,000 people who ate from my little lunch," the boy thought. "How did Jesus do that? Wow! Just because I shared my lunch I got to help with a miracle!"

Based on John 6:1-13

Becoming a Man of God

A man of God shares.

That little boy didn't have any idea that he was going to share in a miracle when he offered his lunch to Jesus. He was willing to share right away when he heard there was a need. He didn't even hold anything back for himself.

How are you at sharing? Do you only share certain things and keep other things for yourself? How do you feel when a friend doesn't share with you?

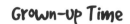

Grown-up Time

Tell your son a sharing story . . . a time when someone shared something special with you. How did it make you feel? How did you feel about the person who shared? How did you feel about sharing with others after that experience?

Encourage your little boy to share generously. Point out a time when you noticed him sharing and tell him how proud you were of him.

A Verse to Remember

Do for others what you would like them to do for you.

Matthew 7:12

Little Man, Big Change

"Out of my way, I want to see Jesus, too." Zacchaeus pushed and shoved, but people wouldn't move out of his way. "What's the matter? Don't you know who I am?" Of course, that was the problem. People did know that Zacchaeus was a cheating tax collector.

"Here he comes," someone shouted. The
crowd moved forward and Zacchaeus was
pushed back against a tree. That gave him
an idea. He scooted up the tree and out on a
big branch. He had a bird's-eye view now.

People shouted at Jesus and begged for his help. Zacchaeus quietly watched the whole thing. When Jesus looked up and said, "Come down, Zacchaeus. I want to come to your house," he nearly fell off his branch.

Zaccheus strutted down the street, making sure everyone saw him. "Ha! Jesus didn't want to come to your houses, did he?"

His attitude made people angry. "Why does Jesus want to go with that creep?" they wondered.

Jesus talked with Zacchaeus and soon the tax collector admitted that he had cheated people. "I promise to pay back the people I cheated. In fact, I'll pay back four times more than I owe!" he promised. Jesus smiled. He knew that Zacchaeus would never be the same. He loved God now!

Based on Luke 19:1-10

Becoming a Man of God

A man of God changes when he meets Jesus.

Zacchaeus was a cheater who didn't have any friends. No one likes a cheat. But when he met Jesus, Zacchaeus saw that he needed to change. He wanted to live the way Jesus wanted him to live.

Are you a pretty nice person? Are there things about you that could be better? Can people watch how you live and see what Jesus is like?

Grown-up Time

Tell your little boy about a time when you
needed to change something in your behavior.
How did you do it? Talk to him about how
people who don't go to church or read the Bible
only know what God's love is like by the way
God's people live and behave.

Talk about some things that each of you could
change in order to be better examples of Christ.
Pray together for help in making those changes.

A Verse to Remember

For God so loved the world that he gave his only
Son, so that everyone who believes in him will
not perish but have eternal life.

John 3:16

Mary's face flushed red and little beads of sweat popped out on her forehead. She felt a knot forming in her stomach and she thought she might faint at any minute. She grabbed a friend's arm to steady herself.

Jesus hoisted the cross onto his shoulder and dragged it down the street. People along the road made fun of him and shouted insults. Mary's heart ached. "Why don't they leave him alone?"

Soldiers threw Jesus to the ground and
nailed his hands and feet to the cross.
When they dropped the
cross into the ground, tears
rolled down Mary's cheeks.
"Come on, King of the Jews, save yourself!"
people shouted.

Mary remembered when the angel told her that her baby was the Messiah and that he would save people from their sins. "That must be what this is all about," she thought.

Even on this terrible day, Jesus' eyes were filled with love. Mary had the oddest feeling when Jesus said, "It is finished." When he died, part of her heart died too. Her son was dead . . . but her Savior would live forever.

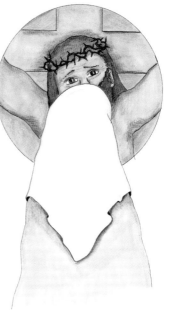

Based on John 19:16-30

Becoming a Man of God

A man of God understands Jesus died on the cross for him.

Jesus left the riches of heaven to come to earth and live as a poor man. He wasn't treated nicely by some people, and they finally killed him on the cross. He died so that our sins can be forgiven and we can someday live in heaven with him.

Have you ever been punished for something you didn't do? How did you feel about it?

Grown-Up Time

Tell your little boy that before Jesus died on
the cross, people had to sacrifice an animal,
such as a sheep or dove, to God before they
could ask him to forgive their sins. Explain
that we don't have to do that anymore
because Jesus died as our sacrifice. Thank him
together for this wonderful gift.

A Verse to Remember
Christ died for everyone.
2 Corinthians 5:14

The Empty Tomb

The sun was just sneaking into the sky when the three women headed to the cemetery. Each was lost in her sad thoughts. All their hopes died when Jesus died. How could they keep on going?

Even in the middle of their pain the women wanted to do the right thing. That's why they were going to put perfumes and oils on Jesus' body. That was the right thing to do, but truthfully, they felt empty and numb.

They walked along in silence until one woman remembered something. "How are we going to move the big stone in front of the tomb?" Several soldiers had strained and pushed to get it in place.

"We'll figure something out," another woman said. When they got to the tomb, they couldn't believe what they saw. The stone was gone! The tomb was open!

One woman went into the tomb and saw
an angel who said, "Jesus isn't here. He came
back to life, just as he told you he would!"

"He's alive!" she called to her friends.
"Praise God, Jesus is alive!"

Based on Mark 16:1-7

Becoming a Man of God
A man of God knows God will do what he says.

The women in this story were sad because they had forgotten what Jesus said he would do. Jesus said he would come back to life, but they weren't expecting that when they went to the tomb.

Has someone ever told you that something would happen, but you didn't believe it? If it did happen, how did you feel?

Grown-up Time

Tell your little boy what some of your childhood hopes were. What are some of your hopes for his future?

Explain that the women at the tomb had given up hope because they didn't believe that Jesus would do what he said. When they found out that he was alive again, they were very happy! Thank Jesus for coming back to life and making a way for us all to be in heaven someday.

A Verse to Remember
You are looking for Jesus, the Nazarene, who was crucified. He isn't here! He has been raised from the dead!
Mark 16:6